45 Ways to Excellent Life

Blythe Ayne, Ph.D.

Books & Audio by Blythe Ayne, Ph.D.

Nonfiction:
Love Is The Answer
45 Ways To Excellent Life
Horn of Plenty — The Cornucopia of Your Life
Life Flows on the River of Love
How to Save Your Life Series:
Save Your Life With The Power Of pH Balance
Save Your Life With The Phenomenal Lemon
Save Your Life with Stupendous Spices

Fiction:
The Darling Undesirables Series:
The Heart of Leo - short story prequel
The Darling Undesirables
Moons Rising
The Inventor's Clone
Heart's Quest

Short Story Collections:
5 Minute Stories
Lovely Frights for Lonely Nights

Children's Illustrated Books:
The Rat Who Didn't Like Rats
The Rat Who Didn't Like Christmas

Poetry:
Home & the Surrounding Territory

CD:
The Power of pH Balance —
Dr. Blythe Ayne Interviews Steven Acuff

45 Ways to Excellent Life

Blythe Ayne, Ph.D.

45 Ways to Excellent Life

Blythe Ayne, Ph.D.

Emerson & Tilman, Publishers
129 Pendleton Way #55
Washougal, WA 98671

All Rights Reserved
No part of this publication may be reproduced, distributed, or transmitted
in any form, or by any means, including photocopying, recording,
or other electronic or mechanical methods, without the prior
written permission of the author, except brief quotations
in critical reviews and other noncommercial
uses permitted by copyright law.

Book & cover design by Blythe Ayne
All Text & Graphics
© 2015-2017 Blythe Ayne

45 Ways to Excellent Life

www.BlytheAyne.com

Paperback ISBN: 978-1-947151-30-7

1. BODY, MIND & SPIRIT/Mindfulness & Meditation
2. BODY, MIND & SPIRIT/Inspiration & Personal Growth
3. BODY, MIND & SPIRIT / General

BIC: FM

Second Edition

45 Ways to Excellent Life

Blythe Ayne, Ph.D.

45 Ways to Excellent Life

Blythe Ayne, Ph.D.

Emerson & Tilman, Publishers
129 Pendleton Way #55
Washougal, WA 98671

All Rights Reserved
No part of this publication may be reproduced, distributed, or transmitted
in any form, or by any means, including photocopying, recording,
or other electronic or mechanical methods, without the prior
written permission of the author, except brief quotations
in critical reviews and other noncommercial
uses permitted by copyright law.

Book & cover design by Blythe Ayne
All Text & Graphics
© 2015-2017 Blythe Ayne

45 Ways to Excellent Life

www.BlytheAyne.com

Paperback ISBN: 978-1-947151-30-7

1. BODY, MIND & SPIRIT/Mindfulness & Meditation
2. BODY, MIND & SPIRIT/Inspiration & Personal Growth
3. BODY, MIND & SPIRIT / General

BIC: FM

Second Edition

DEDICATION:

*To all who desire to manifest
An Excellent Life*

45 Ways to Excellent Life

Table of Contents:

Introduction:		*1*
1	*The Human Hand*	*7*
2	*Stained-Glass Window*	*11*
3	*Goals*	*13*
4	*Observation*	*17*
5	*Excellent!*	*19*
6	*10 Scents*	*23*
7	*Patience*	*25*
8	*Peace*	*29*
9	*Banishing Fear*	*31*
10	*The Mystery Shop*	*35*
11	*Challenges*	*37*
12	*Inhale—Exhale*	*39*
13	*Friendliness*	*41*
14	*Joy*	*45*
15	*Honesty*	*49*
16	*Compliments*	*51*
17	*Positive Outlook*	*55*
18	*Empathy*	*57*
19	*Do*	*59*

20	A Child	63
21	Gratitude	65
22	Metals	68
23	The Child In You	69
24	Character Traits	70
25	The Hero	73
26	The Hero In You	74
27	Interactions	75
28	Challenges	77
29	Animal Magnetism	81
30	Secrets	84
31	Progress	85
32	The Me I See	89
33	Plant Life	91
34	Life Purpose	93
35	Love Your Work	95
36	Train Ride	97
37	Bread Making	99
38	Forgiveness	101
39	A Knock At The Door	105
40	Meditation	107
41	People	110
42	Creators	111
43	Generosity	115
44	Love	119
45	Celebrate!	123

All graphics/photos © Blythe Ayne - previous dates through 2017

Introduction:

Do you ever feel like you're living life waiting for something to happen? There's an almost unformed thought that if only "it"—this illusive something, would just happen, you could finally be happy, or content, or more productive?

What are you waiting for? To fall in love? The kids to leave home? Your boss to treat you better? Your spouse to understand you?

Have you ever heard yourself say, "when such and such happens, I'll finally feel happy, peaceful, joyful, relaxed," or whatever emotion you believe you're longing to feel?

Well, wait no more. Life is *NOW!*

Feeling "on hold" about your life is a self-imposed prison sentence, with you as your own jailer.

45 Ways to Excellent Life is about living without waiting. It's about being more aware, more fulfilled, happier.

I wish you the strength, the will, the autonomy and the determination to bring your dreams—from the simplest to the most complex—into reality.

I believe you can do this by becoming more aware.

One way to become more aware is by actions. Actively involve yourself in one of the meditations in this book each day—or spend any number of days on one if it intrigues you, edifies you and makes your life richer.

Really, actively participate in what you do, involve all your senses—seeing, hearing, tasting, touching, smelling and any sense of sixth sense you may feel, believe, know, or suspect you have. Involve your active thinking, your more contemplative intelligence, your emotions, your psychology, philosophy, spirituality ... all your beliefs and understandings that include, and extend beyond, the six physical sides of yourself.

A very good way to be aware of becoming aware, to nurture your personal autonomy, and to see your growth is to WRITE THINGS DOWN.

So....

Get yourself a blank book. Find one that feels wonderful and comfortable in your hands, that's attractive to look at, but not so precious that you can't bring yourself to write in it.

(I'd like to take an informal survey here—if you have at least one blank book that you've never written in, raise you hand ... the following exercise is especially for you.)

This is a practice exercise that gives you an idea of what **45 Ways to Excellent Life** is all about—Self-Empowerment.

Open The Blank Book

Thumb to any page

Take a pen and make a line from the upper left to the bottom right of the page like this:

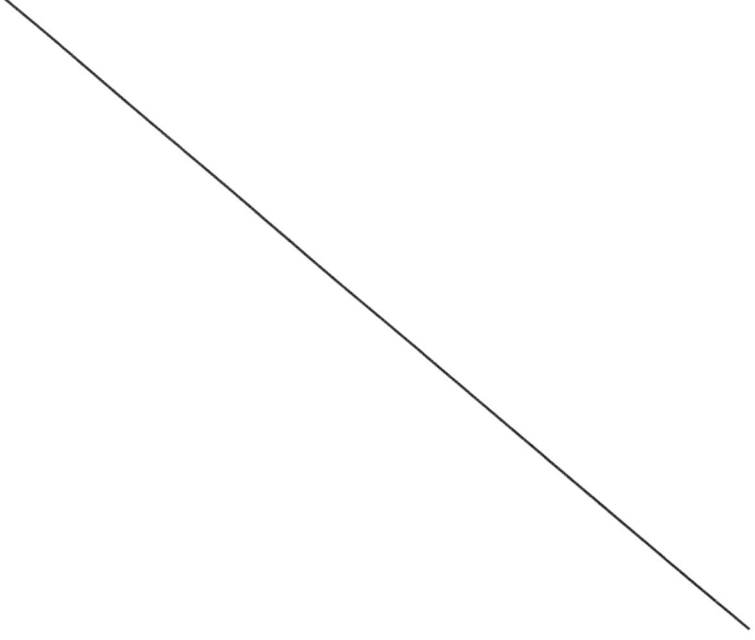

Then make a line from the upper right to the bottom left of the page like this:

You now have this:

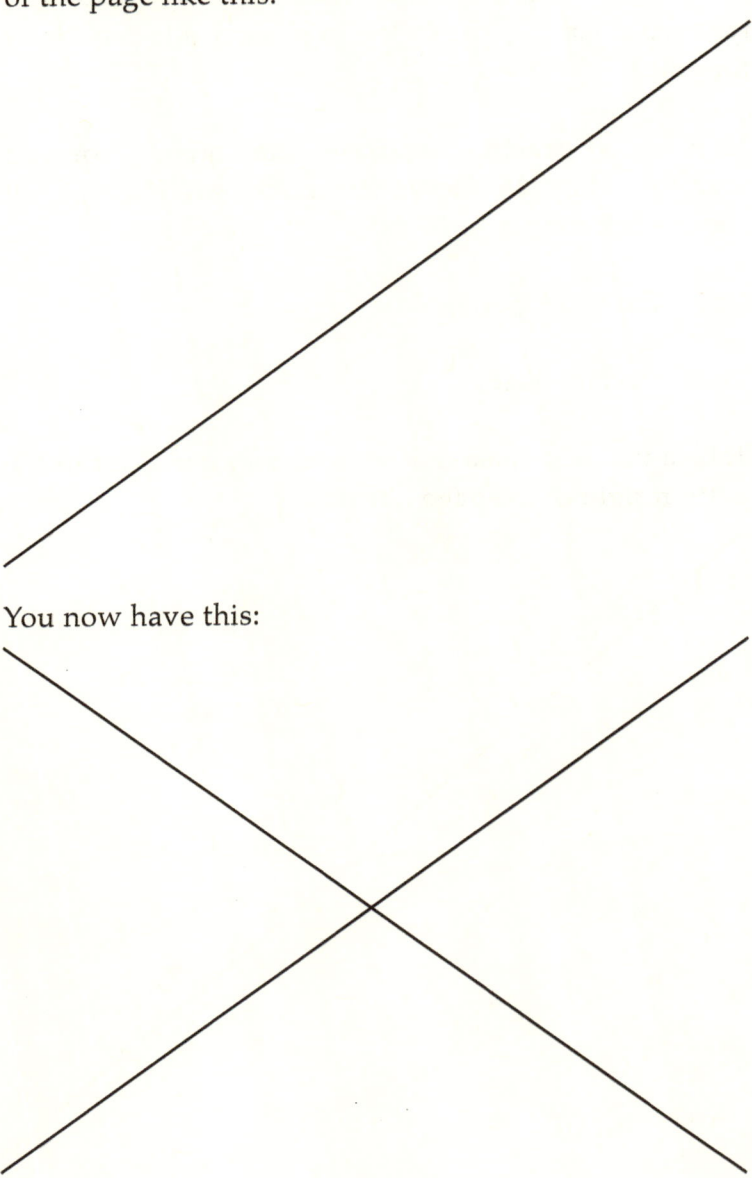

Congratulations—you've just broken the blank-book-is-better-than-me spell!

Date and sign that page.

Now you can go on to write, draw, scratch, scribble, ruminate, cogitate, philosophize, and doodle at will. The book is your safe place. You have power here.

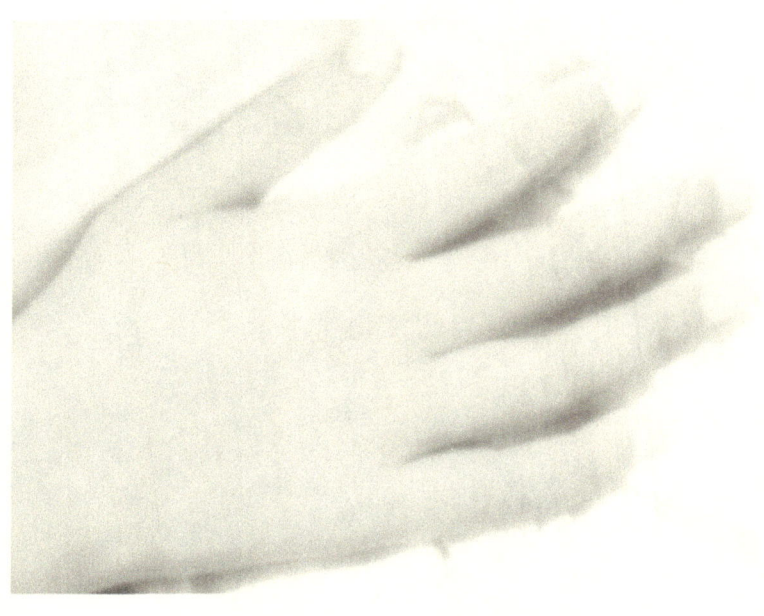

6 · 45 Ways to Excellent Life

1

THE HUMAN HAND

Every moment is full of wonder—for instance, have you ever been taken with how phenomenal an object is the human hand?

The human hand, wonderfully fashioned of twenty-seven bones, and over twenty joints, makes more than one-thousand different movements every day, movements which involve the use of thirty-three muscles, from the forearm into the tips of each finger.

The large muscles in the forearm travel to the fingers through the beautiful, bracelet-like bone structure in the wrist called the carpal tunnel.

In a talk given by Madeline L'Engle, author of *A Wrinkle in Time*, she noted that medical science has discovered that in the soft pads of one's fingertips there is gray cell matter, of the same type that is found in the brain.

She observed that this made excellent sense to her as our fingers are very intelligent. They can read braille, can distinguish the minute shape, texture and substance of things, sight unseen. Our fingers are incredible feeling devices.

> *"The hand is the cutting edge of the mind."*
> **Jacob Bronowski**

Spend time contemplating your hands, appreciating how much they contribute to making life more full and interesting.

Think about all the ways hands contribute to life. Consider all that exists and all that we do because of our hands.

> *"The hand has the richest articulation of space."*
> **Eduardo Chilida**

What are the most wonderful, amazing things that you do with your hands?

What is some amazing thing you could do with your hands that you haven't yet? ... sculpt, paint, play an instrument, make tools, build something, cook, climb a tree, write a novel, write a poem, care for an injured creature ... or?

> *"My hand is the extension of the thinking process and the creative process."*
> **Tadao Ando**

What comes to mind as you contemplate your hands? Write these thoughts and observations down in your book.

2

STAINED-GLASS WINDOW

Find and contemplate a stained-glass window. Spend time alone with the colors of glass and light, consider how each color affects your feelings.

Imagine being the artisan who conceived and created the stained-glass window.

How might the artist's vision have come into mind?

What emotions would the artist feel when the idea first came? when picking out materials? when working with the materials? when the work was first completed? when the work of art was placed in its present location of sharing the vision and creation with others?

Contemplate the light, the different colors, and shades of colors, of the light. What energy, sensation, and/or emotion do you experience from each shaft of light, each animate color?

Every shade of color in the spectrum has its own healing power.

Think of something that is troubling you, or an emotional or physical pain that you have and contemplate this issue while considering each color. You will discover, if you're really engaged in the meditation, that one of the colors of light will abate your troublesome sensation.

Write in your book about what you experience with the lights and your contemplations.

3

GOALS

Napoleon Hill said, "A goal is a dream with a deadline."

What is something you've dreamed, a goal you've had that you have not yet accomplished?

NOW is the time to give that dream a deadline. Begin to give it life and let it breathe by writing it down.

> *Written goals have a way of transforming*
> *wishes into wants; cant's into cans;*
> *dreams into plans; and plans into reality.*
> *Don't just think it - ink it!*
> **Author Unknown**

Little goals make big changes. Big goals are transformative. Don't be shy, cautious, self-critical. Remember, "your heart is always true when it truly speaks to you."

Goals you've not acted upon but that still lay nested quietly hopeful, glowing—and yes, even nagging—in your heart are your gifts to yourself, and potential gifts to the world. Step out bravely. Sometimes the greatest act of bravery is facing one's self, often fond of saying "can't-couldn't-shouldn't."

You Can. You Could. You *MUST!* Own your dream, set a goal.

> *"A goal properly set is halfway reached."*
> **Abraham Lincoln**

I would add to Lincoln's succinct quote that writing a goal, and making a promise to yourself to move toward it, *is* properly setting it.

Dreams that make it into your waking life have had to take a considerable and persevering journey to reach their destination in the three-dimensions. Don't disrespect them by ignoring them or giving them less than your best.

> *"Throw your heart over the fence,*
> *And the rest will follow."*
> **Norman Vincent Peale**

Turn these dreams into achievable goals, and breathe the breath of life into them, one step, one moment, one aspect at a time, until, one day, you'll discover that your dream has become manifest, those goals have been achieved, with new, thrilling goals now on the horizon.

> *"The future belongs to those who believe in the beauty of their dreams."*
> ***Eleanor Roosevelt***

4

OBSERVATION

What is some object in your daily environment that you've never noticed before—a water fountain, a picture on an office mate's wall, a doorway—some taken-for-granted something you've not noticed?

Keep a picture of this object in your mind during the day. Get to know it in your mind, not as much in a concrete way, as in an "I-never-noticed-that-before" way. When you feel tired or stressed during the day, go to the object and consider it in your mind's eye. Breathe deeply while you study this mind's eye image.

Write in your book a brief, objective description of the object.

Then write the subjective description and the subjective experience. Name the object in emotional language ... pretty, unattractive, boring, stimulating, relaxing, stressing, etc., etc. Consider why you've never noticed this object before.

Did you discover that you considered your image of this object while stressed, or when you felt exhausted?

Did you consider it when you were relaxed, calm, happy, energetic?

If you find yourself considering the object in different frames of mind, what do these different experiences feel like?

Was there anything surprising or unknown to you about yourself in these observations and feelings? Write your thoughts and insights in your book.

5

EXCELLENT!

On ten occasions today, say, "things are excellent because _____," and then fill in the blank. Be sure to write these ten occasions in your book.

When we look for excellent experiences, excellent experiences manifest. Turn on a radar focus for the positive, the pleasurable, the constructive, the happy, the caring events, experiences, interactions and inspirations that await in the wings of the stage of your life—they are piled up there in untold heaps, only needing your cue to come out, lovely and edifying, into the spotlight of your life.

Empower Positive Manifestation!

Why not take this one *Way to Excellent Life* into your every day? Wake up every morning with an affirmation of saying ten or maybe twenty, or maybe even more times this day, "This Is *EXCELLENT!*"

For instance, at this very moment, as I'm writing this, I'm in an excellent frame of thinking and feeling. I hear a rustling outside, I step out onto the deck and behold two darling, spotted fawns, with their mother, ten feet ahead of them, looking back at them.

Six eyes immediately look up at me in unison. No one moves, we are all entirely *In The Moment*. Finally one of the fawns resumes grazing, and they return to their deer business, and I return to this page, my day already so excellent, that the rest is delicious frosting (and it's Friday the 13th!).

The more you claim such events, the more they occur.

Trust your excellent life, know your excellent power, and experience your excellent moments!

6

10 SCENTS

Today, completely indulge your Sense of Scent. Name and note down at least ten scents.

Which is your favorite? Why?

Which is your least favorite? Why?

Give some thought to your "why" and write down your personal insights, understandings, and memories.

Recall the emotional component to your liking or disliking a scent, and explore your personal history, remembering the occasions when these scents became meaningful to you.

> *"One scent can be unexpected,*
> *momentary and fleeting,*
> *yet conjure up a childhood summer*
> *beside a lake in the mountains."*
>
> **Diane Ackerman**

The sense of smell is the most memory-evoking/invoking of all our senses. A faint aroma can take us back in time faster than any fictional time-travel machine.

Have you ever found yourself with suddenly a clear mental picture of a moment from your childhood, surprisingly and not consciously called upon? There's a good chance an olfactory input triggered your memory.

A lot of people have an attachment to some pretty funky plastic smells, which hearken back to toy cowboys, soldiers, dolls, or some other beloved Christmas or Birthday toy, long lost and completely forgotten ... well, not completely forgotten, because in the recesses of the mind resides the exact "shape" of that scent.

> *"Nature, exerting an unwearied power,*
> *Forms and gives scent to every flower."*
>
> **William Cowper**

7

PATIENCE

Patience equals calm, and calmness develops a centered self, where you learn the complexities and wonders of who you are, where you develop your special traits, skills and talents—where you clarify your goals and aspirations.

All other endeavors, goals, thoughts, feelings, intentions and intuitions are much more readily accessed and augmented in a general internal environment of patience.

Nurture all the circumstances in which your patience is called upon, whether standing in line, communicating with your family under stressful circumstances, traveling, dealing with a difficult person at work, sorting out your bills, finding yourself in a telephone altercation, or perhaps simply in the process of falling asleep at night.

> *"Adopt the pace of nature; her secret is patience."*
> **Ralph Waldo Emerson**

Buddhist philosophy is helpful in the appreciation of patience. Buddhism notes that everything is impermanent. A lovely moment will pass. An awful moment will pass. Just remain patient, and this moment will segue into another moment, containing another experience.

Every moment and every experience is more meaningful when we are patient within them. The learning, the meaning, rises right to the surface, and if we're patient, we'll be present for that awareness, those observations.

In those terrible moments, the terrible aspect becomes less terrible, while the lovely becomes more lovely.

> *"Genius is eternal patience."*
> *Michelangelo*

Patience is the flowing river upon which flotsam and jetsam cavort in our strange time-bound illusion with the reality of eternity.

Recall an occasion when you were patient, and your patience paid off. Write about this experience in your book. What is an insight you have now, in retrospect, about that occasion of choosing patience?

Practice patience today—add a smile—and notice the positive payoff.

> *"Patience and perseverance have a magical effect, before which difficulties disappear and obstacles vanish."*
> **John Quincy Adams**

8
PEACE

Recipe for Peace:

Sit by water—

A lake, a pond, a stream, a river, the ocean.

Think nothing.

Listen.

Feel.

Smell.

See.

Do this some more.

Start all over again.

Do it longer.

Later, write about this experience in your book.

9

BANISHING FEAR

We all have fears, but our fears keep us from complete, free access to our lives, and ourselves.

Write in your book about at least one specific fear you have. *FACE* it as you have never before. Approach it from all sides. One way to look at a fear is to express it in third-person terms.

Here's an example of a person talking to himself in the third-person: "There was a man who was so afraid of flying that, although he wanted very badly to go to Australia, he knew he never would because he refused to get on a plane."

Then talk to this "other person" as if you have the clearest idea about how he could handle this situation. For instance:

I like this guy quite a lot, and I feel badly that he won't permit himself the wonders of the world because he's chosen to empower his fear more than his desire to see Australia. If I could grant one wish for him, I would wish that he'd see he can choose to be bigger than his fear, and be the boss of it, rather than letting it be the boss of him.

There are several things I could suggest to him. I could suggest:

1. That he talk with someone who is trained in dealing with people's fears.

2. That he do some reading about his fear. There's much helpful information about the fear of flying.

3. That he get books and videos on Australia to create a picture in his mind of being there. I'd tell him that creating a mental picture of doing something is the first step to bringing it into being.

After you've written to your "friend" read what you've written. As you now think about the fact that "he" or "she" is "you," what will you do? Will you follow the advice and suggestions of this friend who has your very best interests at heart? I hope so.

In your life, you will never have a better friend than your *SELF*.

> *"Only when we are no longer afraid do we begin to live."*
> **Dorothy Thompson**

Move forward and live fearlessly, filled and overflowing with a magnificent joy in the present moment, which is where you manifest your life, and is, in truth, the only place you reside.

> *"Don't be afraid to go out on a limb. That's where the fruit is."*
> **H. Jackson Browne**

You may discover you have quite a lot of input when considering your fears. Be sure to have your blank book handy, and write about all the triumphs you experience when becoming the master of your destiny by taking the stuffing out of the bugaboo of fear.

The monster under the bed only gets bigger if we try to pretend it's not there, but it cowers and shrinks when we look under the bed and say *"boo!"*

> *"I'm not afraid of storms, for I'm learning how to sail my ship."*
> **Louisa May Alcott**

10

THE MYSTERY SHOP

Walk into a shop you've never been in. Buy yourself something that captures your fancy, that typically you'd never buy.

Do *NOT* over-think it!

Enjoy the mystery and the unknown when pushing the envelope of your "safe zone" and your usual, routine experiences.

What about that shop intrigued you to enter?

What about the object you bought drew you to it?

What did it feel like to go somewhere you've never been? Interesting? Intimidating? Stimulating?

Write in your book about this experience. Contemplate your emotions and the sensory experience.

What did you see, hear, smell, touch, and maybe even taste that was new and interesting to you?

Was there anything that surprised you, either because you've never encountered it, or, conversely, because it was familiar and you didn't expect to find it in this shop?

One of the best ways we learn is to encounter something new and different. We often tend to name things and then dismiss them. It is wise to enter the unknown on occasion, to remember the thrill of learning.

11

CHALLENGES

Enjoy challenges!

What puts more energy into life than challenges?

Challenge is defined as "a stimulating task or problem," (Merriam-Webster).

Let's put emphasis on "stimulating," because without stimulation, a task is just a chore, and a problem is just an annoyance. But if it's stimulating, then it's challenging. The gauntlet has been thrown down! Life calls you to action!

You are lured into the labyrinth, so bring along your knowledge, intellect, training, skills, talents, feelings, and intuitions to find your way out and to arrive at a solution ... this journey is, indeed, stimulating.

> *"Mountains cannot be surmounted
> except by winding paths."*
> **Johann Wolfgang Von Goethe**

Recall, now, a challenge you've shied away from, or ignored, or attempted to foist off upon someone else. Today, enter the labyrinth, engage your awesome intellect, talents, emotions, intuition—see how well fortified you are?—and take on this challenge. It'll be stimulating, and you'll learn something you did not know before.

Write about this challenge in your book. Write at least three steps you are going to take upon entering the labyrinth in order to discover your way to the stimulating solution.

> *"I wanted to feel unsure again.
> That's the only way I learn,
> the only way I feel challenged."*
> **Connie Chung**

12

INHALE—EXHALE

Here's an exercise you can do every day:

Inhale — Exhale….

In with what you desire
Out with what you don't want.

Make a very clear mental image of what you desire to call into your life, and a very clear image of what you're ready to release.

In — I am claiming peace
Out — I am releasing confusion

In — I am becoming more mindful
Out — I release living in an unaware state

In — I choose to be happy
Out — I release anger, pain, guilt

In — I am claiming my Heart's Desire
Out — I am releasing all blocks and impediments to my goals and intentions

You will bring events, objects and people into into your life—and positive emotional states of being—when you breath in what you desire, and breath out what you release. You'll may find it interesting to observe that the more you really, truly desire something, the more you'll breathe in what you claim and exhale what you release.

Breathe Deeply!

Record and date in your book what you are calling into your life.

13

FRIENDLINESS

Write in your book about your relationship with friendliness. Recall the events of a recent experience you've had as a result of extending your friendliness, and record the story in your book.

Imagine the pleasure it will give you—once again!—when you stumble upon this little vignette some time in the future.

Lack of friendliness may be central to much of life's discontent, as what we send out is what tends to return. If ever you have a gnawing sensation of being disliked, engage your authentic friendliness, and see if the energy doesn't turn right around.

An unfriendly, emotionally negative place is so much more expensive than the results are worth. Being kind, considerate, and helpful will result in people being kind, considerate and helpful in return, and they are doing so because they authentically like you and desire to contribute to your happiness.

Even if that were not so, the *Realm of Friendliness* is still a more emotionally satisfying, strengthening, and pleasant place to be, as we radiate good will and love to all.

14
JOY

Discovering Joy.

No matter what unanticipated curves life may throw you, as long as you acknowledge, name, and are familiar with your essential inner joy, you will maintain your equilibrium.

Thich Nhat Hanh said, "Sometimes your joy is the source of your smile, but sometimes your smile can be the source of your joy."

Have you discovered this yet? Consciously wear a smile all day. While driving the car, staring at a computer screen, mowing the lawn, scolding the kids, on the phone resolving a muddled bill, recalling the past, thinking of the future, being entirely and wholly in the moment ... whatever the case may be, consciously and repeatedly, exercise your smile-joy muscles.

> *"Joy is the feeling of grinning inside."*
> **Melba Colgrove**

I believe that joy is among the deepest bedrock, of positive emotions, along with peace. We may not always be happy-happy-happy .... but if in essence you have joy, you will, sooner or later, find your happiness nesting within it, waiting for an occasion to burst forth.

Joy is the authentic emotion that takes pleasure—real, true, empathic pleasure—in other people's happiness and success.

> *"One of the sanest and most generous*
> *joys of life comes from being happy*
> *over the good fortune of others."*
> **Robert A. Heinlein**

Joy is not greedy, impatient, woeful, angry, aggressive, hateful, prejudiced, jealous, or mean-spirited.

Joy manifests in the opposite of all of those—joy is generous, patient, happy, tolerant, loving, has no prejudice, and is purely spiritual.

Joy is the continual calling of our higher self to the three-dimensional being, which is living this life in an apparent, but false, separation.

Joy resides in infinity, but fully understands the finite continuum of time and space, and joy therefore knows that all sorrows, fears and griefs are transient, and by the nature of their transience, they are, ultimately, unreal.

> *Joy is a net of love by which you can catch souls."*
> **Mother Teresa**

The second part of today's *Way to Excellent Life* is to write in your book all the ways you experienced joy today. If you wear a smile all day, you will receive many smiles back, and each of those is an individual joy.

Acknowledging joy is the most amazing, and yet simple, way of making joy. Discover your joy by making joy, and make your joy by discovering it.

> *"Joy delights in Joy."*
> **William Shakespeare**

The third part of today's *Way to Excellent Life* is to write in your book "Joy Moments" you recall from your past. Be generous and joy-filled as you consider joyous occasions in your personal history.

> *Joy is not in things; it is in us."*
> **Richard Wagner**

The fourth part of today's *Way to Excellent Life* is to write in your book joys you see manifesting in your future. Name them, honor them, give them breath and reality by imagining them right now, and calling them to you.

Keep in mind the energy in the word IMAGINING:
    image = seeing
    ing   = bringing into being

Then be sure to enter and date the joy when it manifests, when that future becomes the ever rising "now."

> *"Joy is the holy fire that keeps our purpose warm and our intelligence aglow."*
> ***Helen Keller***

15

HONESTY

Honesty is an essential character trait. To have a completely *Excellent Life*, honesty is at its center. This includes honesty with strangers, your employer, your friends and relatives, and especially your spouse and children.

You are always role modeling for your children. If you think you're fooling your spouse and children when you're dishonest, think again. People may not know what the exact truth is, but they *do* know when they're receiving an untruth. This is another of those events which ultimately we will receive back with the karma boomerang, which can be quite unpleasant when on the receiving end.

So for one day, tell your unvarnished truths. If you're a naturally candid person, you may get to take the day off with simply reflecting on the benefits of honesty.

For others, this exercise may feel quite challenging, if not downright occasionally rude. But if you find you can't tell the truth, then don't speak. Even though this may be an untruth by omission, at least you haven't compounded untruth. The objective is to get an understanding about how much of a gap you have between what you speak and what you feel or believe.

At the same time, temper this exercise with the realization that truth is a subjective experience, and is sometimes very different from objective facts. That is to say, there is no need to be rude or unkind, and if you discover your truths are unkind or judgmental, you may want to begin to shift your underlying energy.

This experience asks that you explore your own ideas around what you say is truth. Then honor others' truths as your would have them honor yours.

16

COMPLIMENTS

Mark Twain said, "I can live for two months on a good compliment."

I completely agree. In fact, some of the smallest compliments I ever received, even as a child, I have remembered word for word my entire life ... is this not true for you also?

Do yourself and the world a favor ... pass it on!

Today give at least five compliments. If this is something you already do, double the number.

If, on the other hand, this is new to you, consider that positive reinforcement is like gas in a machine. You may be a hard worker, you may have the best of intentions, but unless you give gas to the workings of your machinery, and compliments to those around you, you're going to be stuck.

> *"We underestimate the power of a kind word, a listening ear, an honest compliment, or the smallest act of caring, all of which have the potential to turn a life around."*
> **Leo F. Buscaglia**

Is there anyone you particularly admire? Think about how that person interacts with others. Hugely successful people give compliments. They reinforce individuals where they are, perhaps even in the process of imparting a helpful critique. It's not difficult to see the positive effect of positive reinforcement.

You may have been socialized in a family that did not give compliments, and so it doesn't come readily to do so.

If this is the case for you, let me share a secret ... when you are generous with compliments, the person who feels the very best about it is YOU. Be ridiculously generous with authentic compliments and see if your experience doesn't prove this to be true ... not to mention that the compliment boomerang will return the same wonderful experience to you!

> *"A compliment is verbal sunshine."*
> **Robert Orben**

At first, handing out compliments may be difficult. It may feel unnatural. It may even seem forced, fake, inauthentic, because it is not something you were taught. If you grew up in a critical environment, it may very well look like being critical is your assignment.

This is a faulted assignment.

You may wish to argue that you're simply telling people the truth (the usual litany of people who must criticize). You may feel certain about the truth of the criticisms you imparting to others, but the *FACT* remains that you are not making the other person feel better. And so they are not likely to be motivated to implement the suggestions contained in your criticism nearly as much as if you were complimentary, acknowledging where the person is and who they are in the most reinforcing manner you can.

At the end of the day, reflect on all the compliments you gave, and—and here's the important part—the reactions you received.

You may not have received a response from everyone, because many people have been socialized in a critiquing environment, and do not know how to respond to compliments. But write that response down also, so you can see the harm relentless criticism does to the highest of human feelings and expression.

As you continue employing this *Way to Excellent Life*, you will observe that quite a collection of warm responses are accruing under the heading of "Compliments I Gave."

> *"A spoonful of sugar makes*
> *the medicine go down."*
> **Mary Poppins**

17

POSITIVE OUTLOOK

Support and embellish your positive outlook on life—not only will you feel better, but you'll notice those around you respond very favorably to your positive outlook.

Simply encourage the positive side of any situation or event. Kind, encouraging words make positive things occur. People like to be around positive people.

Think positively and masterfully and life becomes richer in experience and achievement."
Edward Rickenbacker

The universe responds to our energy. As Jack Canfield advises, it's a good and advantageous idea to experience "pronoia," which is the opposite of paranoia. Imagine that the universe and people are all conspiring to do you good!

Write in your book a scene of pronoia ... a situation in which you see the universe—by whatever means—plotting to do you good.

Tell the whole story, flesh it out, right up to and including the happy ending when you see yourself with a most pleasant and desirable result.

> *"The positive thinker sees the invisible, feels the intangible, and achieves the impossible."*
> ***Author Unknown***

18

EMPATHY

Remember exercise number 10 when you walked into a shop and bought yourself something you'd never typically buy? Recall the item or retrieve it and put it before you.

What are the qualities, character, looks, beliefs, clothing, profession, hobbies, disappointments, morals, spiritual beliefs, aspirations, fears, convictions, disappointments, height, weight, co-workers, friends, children, siblings, mother and father of the person who would walk into that shop and buy this object, purposefully and with intention?

Unlike you, that person specifically wanted this item.

Feel compassion, empathy, insight, love and understanding for this person.

In other words, *be*, in your imagination, this other person.

In your book write about your insights in considering what it is like to "be" someone else. This other person may be completely hypothetical. Or someone you know may suddenly come to mind—either way, really crawl inside the skin and mind of this other person and write from that perspective.

19
DO

Don't let anyone tell you that you can't do something!

Explore your facets. If something intrigues you, *do it*. Accepting someone else's projection of defeat may cause you to miss the very thing you're attuned to, the very thing that is your purpose.

If it turns out not to be "your thing," then that's simply another discovery. What do you have to lose? Why spend your life saying, "I could have ...?" Say instead, "*I did!*" There's no such thing as failure, there's only learning.

> *"All life is an experiment. The more experiments you make, the better."*
> **Ralph Waldo Emerson**

Write in your book about something you have allowed someone else to have influence over you to the degree that you put it down and walked away from it.

Now recall your first passion or desire about that interest or activity. Remember how you felt before you permitted someone else's influence to contaminate it. Re-own your thoughts, emotions, and bodily sensations attached to this Heart's Desire, and engage in it again as if it were brand new.

Inspirations, fascinations, beliefs that you can do something or desires to learn something are not accidents or mere whimsey, they are the whisperings of your higher self, calling to you to have the fullest, most meaningful, most creative and wonderful life experiences that you can possibly imagine, and even beyond what you can imagine.

> *"You must do the thing you think you cannot do."*
> **Eleanor Roosevelt**

Write about this renewed claim, and date it. Observe how your thoughts and feelings change when you think about this activity on your own terms without any external influence. You may notice an expansive, even excited, feeling opening inside you. Own this lovely precious feeling, which is yours and yours alone.

Imagine all the things that exist in our present reality that were originally considered fantastic, impossible imaginings—airplanes, space rockets, television and telephones are but a few obvious ones.

Just a few short years ago certain advances in medicine were considered beyond impossible. Even a cell phone was, until not that long ago, science fiction.

How much have artists, writers, poets and performers opened the windows of our minds, and allowed us to see further than we ever have before?

Therefore, hold in highest regard your inspirations and creative passions.

> *"To dream the impossible dream ....*
> *To reach the unreachable star ....*
> *This is my quest, to follow that star ....*
> **Joe Darion**
> *lyrics from* **The Impossible Dream**

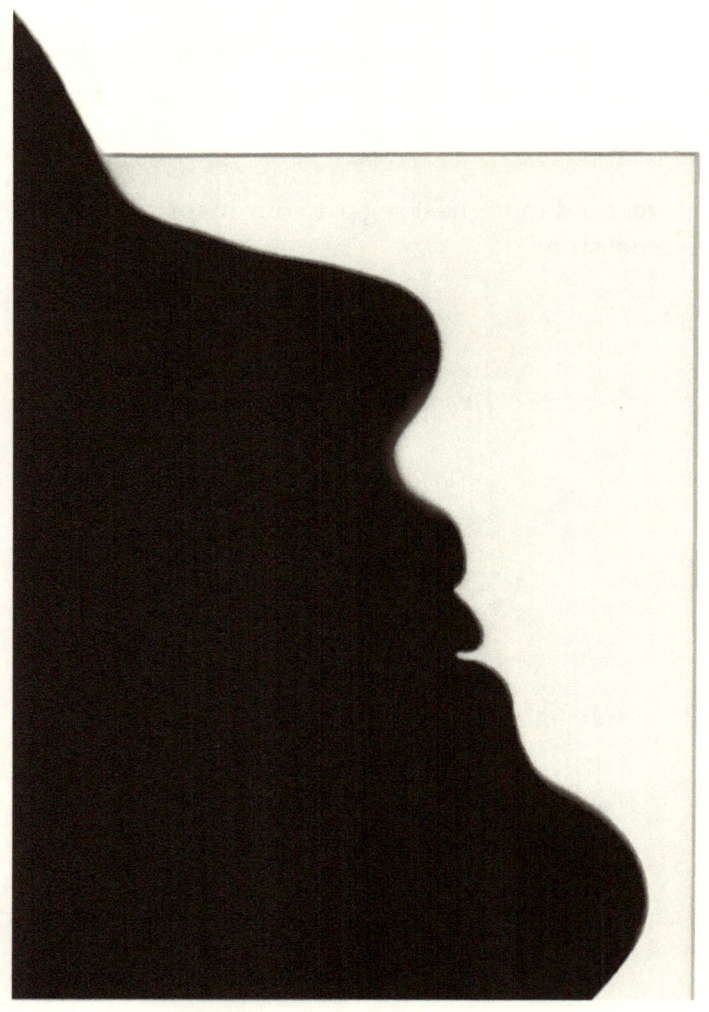

20

A CHILD

Bring to mind a child you know. Write, being as descriptive as you can, about the following:

What does the child's voice sound like?

What color are the child's eyes?

What color is the child's hair?

What color is the child's skin?

What does the child wonder about?

What does the child need?

What does the child desire?

What does the child fear?

What does the child love?

What does the child imagine about the future?

What's the child's understanding of life?

What takes the child's complete attention? Why?

Give this child your undivided wonderment.

21

GRATITUDE

Dr. Masaru Emoto, who wrote the amazing book, **Messages from Water**, and whose work was featured in **What the Bleep Do We Know?** stated that he believes gratitude is an even greater emotion than love.

I pondered this when I heard him say it in a workshop I attended. I came upon the understanding that gratitude seems to be love in motion. I have love and my response to that love is a movement in me, a feeling, which is gratitude.

However it may seem to you, what remains is that there is great peace and power in gratitude. How wonderful it feels to be filled with gratitude.

How pleasurable to wake up in the morning and hear the birds singing and say, "thank you!" or to see a rainbow and say "thank you!" To eat and say, "thank you!"

All amazing blessings, are they not?

What a blessing to be able to move through every day, filled with gratitude, overflowing with the joy and excitement which real, true gratitude produces.

> *"Wake at dawn with a winged heart and give thanks for another day of loving."*
> **Kahlil Gibran**

Write in your book today three things about which you feel gratitude. The first one is something that you are knowingly thankful for every day.

The second one is something you have not thought about in some while in terms of gratitude. Maybe it's something/someone you've come to take for granted. Consciously take the trip from granted to gratitude.

The third one is something you see manifesting in your future, or that you are in the process of laying claim to in the future. Express gratitude for that event or experience as though it were here today and now.

Of course you need not limit your Gratitudes to three ... you can fill up all the books you can lay your hands on with attitudes of gratitude.

Watch for a change deep inside you. It's so amazing to express gratitude whenever anything catches our intellect, stimulates our emotions, delights our fancy, or even, simply, provides for our essential day to day living.

You will fairly glow from the inside out when making this your constant perspective.

> *"Gratitude makes sense of our past, brings peace for today, and creates a vision for tomorrow."*
> **Anonymous**

22

METALS

Consider the properties of a metal—silver, gold stainless steel, platinum, pewter, copper, brass, nickel, etc. Imagine the molecules inside, how they're arranged, think about how the metal you've chosen to contemplate today gets its color. Recall its appearance, how it feels, bring to mind how it smells.

Metals are everywhere in our life experience—jewelry, pots and pans, automobiles, machinery, medical and scientific equipment, the rebar and other metal components of our homes, schools and work places.

Metals, humming with energy, form an infrastructure to our lives that we rarely consider. Contemplate all the places where metals are your staid servant, making life safer, prettier and more convenient.

Write in your book the thoughts and feelings that come up.

23

THE CHILD IN YOU

In number 20 *Way to Excellent Life*, the life and wonderment of a child was contemplated.

What power in a new mind! All of creation is becoming and unfolding in a child. Write in your book about each of the aspects that you explored in that child, now, about yourself as a child.

Pick a specific age and picture yourself at that age. Then have a conversation with that child you as you answer the questions from number 20.

Search your *self* for the child in you ... great power waits to unfold.

24

CHARACTER TRAITS

Develop your positive character traits.

Benjamin Franklin carried with him 13 cards, and on each one he had written a positive character trait that he considered essential to a good and fulfilled life.

Every day he would work with conscious intention on the character trait written on the card of the day.

On the following pages you'll find his list, which includes his brief notations regarding each trait.

Which of these traits resonate with you? Write them in your book, and include your own thoughts regarding what that trait means to you, how it applies to who you are, and how it contributes to the growth you're embarked upon.

Benjamin Franklin's 13 Virtues:

Personal:

Temperance: Eat not to dullness, drink not to elevation.

Order: Let all your things have their places.

Resolution: Resolve to perform what you ought, perform what you resolve.

Frugality: Waste nothing.

Moderation: Avoid extremes.

Industry: Lose no time, be usefully engaged, cut off unnecessary actions.

Cleanliness: In body, clothes, and habitation.

Tranquility: Be not disturbed at trifles.

Social:

Silence: Speak not but what may be of benefit to others or yourself.

Sincerity: Use no hurtful deceit, think innocently and justly.

Justice: Wrong none by doing injuries.

Chastity: Never use venery to the injury of your own or another's peace or reputation.

Humility: Imitate Socrates and Jesus.

I would add additional role models, such as the Dalai Lama and Mother Teresa.

25

THE HERO

Imagine you are about to meet the one person in all of time you would like to meet more than any other person.

Who is it?

What about this person holds fascination for you?

Picture the perfectly comfortable situation in which you are meeting. Describe in your book the location, environment, and the person in detail.

Write the five burning questions you would ask this person, given such a remarkable opportunity.

26

THE HERO IN YOU

Now answer the five questions you would ask the hero yourself. Just let the writing flow from you freely, without judgment or hesitation. Free writing allows you to tap into both what your subconscious knows and what your higher self knows. This information is typically unavailable to the conscious, ego self.

Believe and know that you can access the answers to your greatest questions.

27

INTERACTIONS

Life is about interacting with others. We are a social creature and an *Excellent Life* has many interactions. We need others—from the cashier at the grocery store, to our coworkers, to our friends, to our family.

Life is fraught with endless tacit and overt agreements, which, at base, address needs. You need the person driving at a right angle to you to stop at his red light, not to ignore it and broadside you. You need to know that your employer recognizes your services this week and will pay you for them. You need to know that your spouse cares about you and that the goals you've discussed are shared.

Write about your favorite relationships with others.

Why are you comfortable with these relationships? What about these particular relationships is healthy?

Where, if anywhere, can you contribute to make the relationship even stronger, neither neglectful nor codependent?

Are there any strong, healthy relationships that you do not have, that you desire to? Describe this relationship in detail in your book.

28

CHALLENGES

Today, watch for someone in a challenging and disagreeable interaction with another who chooses to handle the situation with uncommon grace.

How is that person handling negative energy?

Is there *entanglement* or is there *engagement*?

Is there *reaction* or *response*?

Is there *increased muddle* or movement toward *clarification*?

Is it *"it's all about me"* or *"I understand your position"*?

Sometimes, when experiences tax us, we respond with simply shutting down with apathy, which, of course, allows for no solutions, while the opposite of apathy is entanglement, which also provides no solution.

> "I do not at all understand the mystery of grace, only that it meets us where we are and does not leave us where it found us."
> **Anne Lamott**

Think about the challenge of sitting down with a pile of strings of Christmas lights in a jumble. It's easy to want to get up and walk away, and it's not surprising if one were to feel frustration and potentially end up entangling the lights even more.

But, of course, there's only one solution to untangling jumbled up strings of lights and that's to sit down, find an end and unknot the lights, light by light, engaging in the project at hand with focus. Engagement is where we are neither apathetic nor entangled, and it calls upon grace in order to be most effective.

Is there *response* or *reaction*? If you *respond* to what's needed, in this case, calmly working to the next light, the string will ultimately become free and untangled.

Reaction, on the other hand, such as shaking the lights and heaping bad language upon the lights (i.e., invoking negative energy that only augments the jumble) does not get to the goal of untangled lights and, in fact, may damage them, defeating the entire project.

As long you have *engagement* and *response* there will be movement toward clarity and meaningful resolution.

If the response to the jumble is self-oriented—it's all about me, or mine, or ours—how can there be an untangled resolution? But if you are inspired by empathy (wherein you say and you *feel*, "I understand your position") the lights stand a chance of providing us all—those we agree with and those with whom we have a differing opinion or belief—with the pleasure of untangled, unbroken, glowing lights!

Write about your observations of a person handling a challenge with grace. Perhaps that person was you!

> *"Grace is available for each of us every day, but we've got to remember to ask for it with a grateful heart and not worry about whether there will be enough for tomorrow."*
> **Sarah Ban Breathnach**

29

ANIMAL MAGNETISM

If you have a cat or dog, get down on the creature's level and have a good talk. Look into those wonderful eyes and really contemplate that creature's life.

If you've never talked to your pet in this interactive way, you may discover she appears to be nervous, and she probably is. Animals are intelligent and careful about behavior that's unfamiliar. Respect her fears and caution. You might want to win her over by giving her more interactive attention. Your life will be richer for it.

If you're already highly interactive with your canine/feline friend, take it a step further. Consider his intelligence, his emotions—likes, dislikes, fears, comforts.

Hold him and feel him breathe—in ... out ... in ... out. Visualize the blood coursing through his body, and the delicate bones of his torso, legs, head. Appreciate how wonderfully contrived he is. Smell his fur, and, fragrant or otherwise, take it in.

Look around you and consider what life is like from your animal friend's perspective.

What are the things he most readily sees? No wonder he jumps up on the bed/sofa/counters/furniture! Okay, maybe he doesn't do that. But was there a time when you had to train him to stop by "doggedly" reminding him that the penalty of being up there was greater than whatever reward he got from being at that level?

If you don't have a cat or a dog, get to know one, even if you have to meet a dog waiting outside a coffee shop for her master. Don't force yourself on a dog who doesn't trust you, obviously, but many dogs are open to a bit of discussion at a polite distance, and many dog owners are flattered when you find their dog more charming than all those others.

The same exchange can be negotiated with a cat, although they aren't as easy to find. After all, they don't typically sit around waiting for anyone!

Once you've introduced yourself to your new cat or dog acquaintance, look deeply into her eyes, see the intelligence, sense her mood/emotions. Consider her life in this environment—restaurant food, busy streets, lots of other cat/dog acquaintances, human strangers talking to you.

Expand your awareness of animal intelligence and personality, while considering the world at nine inches to three feet off the ground. An animal's intelligence is not inferior—but it is very different.

Being species-centric is limiting. Opening your awareness to other creatures expands your appreciation of life.

And opening our minds in any way increases intelligence as we give the gray matter exercise.

Write in you book about your inter-species insights.

30
SECRETS

There's a machine that reveals secrets.

What would it reveal about you?

What does this secret mean?

Why do you feel this piece of information needs to be hidden?

How does this secret-keeping feel?

Write your insights in your book.

31

PROGRESS

Perfection Versus Progress

You don't have to be Perfect. But it's good to be aware.

Many people have ideas and notions around perfection that get in the way of their progress.

I've worked with many, many individuals who have a dream, an aspiration, inspiration, invention, book, performance, insight, knowing, so on and so forth, and yet, though they talk about it all the time, they never take action to bring it into being.

A major road block is often one's picture of perfection. That is to say, the strange belief that one must, somehow, be perfect, and that one's creation must spring into being, full blown, also perfect.

But, as Geoffrey F. Fisher has observed, "When you aim for perfection, you discover it's a moving target."

As you learn about the field where your interests lie, you discover that the more you look, the more you see.

This is the point at which I've heard people begin to mutter a variety of predictable phrases such as, "My idea has already been done, I'm not going to work on it any more," or "There are people who know a lot more about my subject than I do. Who do I think I am?"

Or, conversely, "There doesn't seem to be any information on the subject of my interest, I guess I'm the only one who thinks about this, why bother."

And other defeating, negative affirmations.

To which I respond, "Get in motion and create your creation! You have an inspiration, what business is it of yours to be judgmental about it? Get out of the way and let the information that's trying to come through you *come through.*"

You never know how your inspiration may affect, have meaning for, help, or give pleasure to others (and yourself!). You never know where your work may hit home, may change lives, may reach someone only you might reach.

Every snowflake has its own shape, how much more true is this of you?

> *"Give up on being perfect and begin the work of becoming yourself."*
> **Anna Quindlen**

For today's *Way to Excellent Life,* contemplate something you've wanted to bring into being, where you've allowed misconceptions surrounding perfection to interfere.

Move out all the limiting road blocks and begin by writing in your book a description of the idea, the story, book, invention, or creation of any sort, that you have discovered inside yourself.

Give it life and believe in your inspiration.

> *"Perfectionism is the enemy of creation."*
> **John Updike**

32

THE ME I SEE

Today, spend time considering the "ME" you see, and your "ME" that others see.

Open your book to two facing blank pages. Title the left page "The 'ME' Others See," and the right page "The 'ME' I See."

Now, begin jotting down aspects of yourself that are as you see you, and aspects of yourself that are how you believe others see you. You might have some of the same things on both pages, you might not. Come up with at least ten items for each page.

Now mark a plus beside any that are positive and a minus beside any that are negative.

Do you have any minuses?

Are they only on one side, or on both sides?

Contemplate these minuses and ask yourself if they're objectively true, or if you're being unnecessarily hard on yourself when you could be kinder.

What if you were your best friend? Imagine what you would say if these negatives were directed at your friend.

Perhaps this exercise points up a particular area that you can lay claim to. Remember, you don't have to be all "nice." In fact, being "nice" might be something you *see as a minus!*

The goal of this *Way to Excellent Life* is personal empowerment in either reframing negative thoughts you have of yourself into positives, or changing negative habits into positive behaviors.

33

PLANT LIFE

Today's *Way to Excellent Life* is to spend some time studying a plant. Any plant—house plant, weed, flower, garden vegetable.

What are the leaves like—rounded, spiky, symmetrical on the stem, asymmetrical? What is its color?

What kind of green, brown, orange?

What is its scent like?

How does it feel—soft, fuzzy, slick, sticky?

Can you see veins in the leaves?

What's your favorite thing about this leaf?

What's your favorite thing about the plant it comes from?

What, if anything, do you not like about it?

Write in your book about any discoveries you made about the plant.

Did the experience trigger memories? Write them down.

Did your mind "wander"? To where? Why?

You might tape or paste the leaf in your book. You could fill up the whole blank book with your thoughts about this leaf, if you desired to.

34

LIFE PURPOSE

I have had many people ask me, in the course of my working with them, "what is my purpose?"

This unfailingly surprises me, because we've already been working on their purpose. Since I know their purpose, as they have told me what it is perhaps numerous times—apparently without hearing themselves—we must then begin the work of getting them to realize what I've already been told by them, without my shocking them too much by flat-out telling them.

This can sometimes be very long, circuitous, even exhausting work, because, for whatever reasons, people resist what they know about their purpose, and often express not "being worthy" of their own gifts. I have many, many times said, "get out of your way!"

People accept as their due a rusted, secondhand bike,

and refuse to accept the shiny, new, perfectly-working, one with their name printed on the frame, and in their favorite color, They constantly walk around it and stumble over it in order to get to the rusted, second-hand, bike.

> *"The purpose of life is a life of purpose."*
> **Robert Byrn**

I suspect you, too, know your purpose. Don't waste time and energy wondering what it is. It is that which calls to you, it is that which haunts you, waking and sleeping. Never mind if some voice in you says this aspiration is too big for you. That is the voice of defeat, and the *Way to Excellent Life* sidesteps defeat, ignores defeat, does not have time to listen to defeat!

Write your purpose in your book today, no holds barred. Dare to fashion it in all its magnificent detail. Believe that you and your purpose are one, and your *Being* will begin to manifest your purpose in your *doings*. One step at a time, *In the Moment!*

> *"Don't waste life in doubts and fears, invest yourself in the work before you, well assured that the right performance of this hour's duties will be the best preparation for the ages that follow."*
> **Ralph Waldo Emerson**

35

LOVE YOUR WORK

ork hard and love it.

Write in your book about hard work that you love.

36

TRAIN RIDE

In your mind, take a train ride. Get off at your favorite destination.

Write in your book what you find there. What makes this your favorite place?

What is the environment like?

What do you see around you?

What is the culture like in this place?

Is there anyone waiting for you, or is this a great adventure you're taking alone?

Write in your book about your amazing train ride, and what you learned on this trip.

37

BREAD MAKING

ake bread.

If you've never made bread, don't let the lack of experience have anything to do with this *Way to Excellent Life*.

Make bread for the sensory delight. Feel the texture of the flour and yeast and oil and water squishing through your fingers. Take your rings off and let the kid-in-you enjoy these gooshy, primal sensations. Feel the dough responding and firming with your kneading.

Work what you need into your kneading. Throughout the centuries bread makers have balanced their energies by working out pain, iniquities, trials, troubles, tribulations, and the injustices of life upon the accepting, pliant kneaded bread dough.

In this meditative state, one can discover mental balance, realize solutions to problems, or become patient with the insoluble, working it all out on the staff of life.

And, as if all this was not enough, you're not through yet with the sensory delights that bread making provides. Next the baking bread works its aromatic alchemy from within in the oven. You, the bread maker, can sit with your book, enjoying every moment of this creative experience, writing it all down.

How lovable life is!

> *"The smell of good bread baking, like the sound of lightly flowing water, is indescribable in its evocation of innocence and delight."*
> **M. F. K. Fisher**

38

FORGIVENESS

Forgiveness is today's *Way to Excellent Life*. First and foremost, forgiveness heals *you*. When you say, "I cannot forgive the other," you are wounding yourself anew, again and again, every time you say it.

Forgiveness, over time, also heals the other. That is to say, eventually the other is likely to learn what the deed that needs forgiveness felt like to you. But even if, by chance, this never happens, you are healed and have moved on.

> *"To forgive is to set a prisoner free and discover that the prisoner was you."*
> **Lewis B. Smede**

Forgiveness comes from an understanding that we are all human, from realizing that in this life we've all done something to another that was hurtful or caused pain, although we may never have intended it. We have all merited receiving forgiveness.

So, even if someone has harmed or hurt you in a way you would never do to anyone, it is both intelligent and a display of a high EQ—emotional quotient—to forgive, sincerely and completely.

> *"Forgiveness isn't colored with expectations that the other person apologize or change.*
> *Love them and release them.*
> *Life feeds back truth to people in its own way and time."*
> **Sara Paddington**

Bring to mind, now, an occasion that still festers, a sliver in you heart, where you have not relinquished the hold someone has upon you, because you've not forgiven that person or persons for an act that trespassed upon you.

What is the payoff to you to harbor this anger, resentment, frustration, pain and non-forgiveness? Is it about "getting" to feel sorry for yourself?

This is the perfect moment to learn that if you allow yourself to be a victim, which is what non-forgiveness nurtures, you will always encounter victimizers.

The emotional hold of non-forgiveness leaves a gaping wound in our energy field that is absolutely attractive to victimizing energy. Heal yourself and move on.

> *"The weak can never forgive.*
> *Forgiveness is the attribute of the strong."*
> **Mahatma Gandhi**

Write in your book about this experience with forgiveness. You might want to leave a bit of space, because it's highly probable that you will have additional insights in the coming days if you make this forgiving shift in your essential energy.

> *"Forgiveness enlarges the future."*
> **Paul Boese**

39

A KNOCK AT THE DOOR

Imagine you hear a knock at the door—who's on the other side?

Why is this person there?

What's your reaction?

How do you feel about this person at your door?

Write it all down in your book.

40

MEDITATION

 book about various *Ways to Excellent Life* would not be complete if it didn't address *Meditation*.

There is no wrong way to meditate, there are only effective ways to meditate and more effective ways to meditate.

Meditation is about finding that quiet place within you. It resides in all of us, although to some people this seems not true. It is, then, perhaps helpful to have some other concepts of meditation that will help you find your quiet spot.

Meditation is what makes music out of your life, just as the spaces between the notes is what makes music out of sounds.

Perhaps a bit ironically, if there are just sounds, no matter how lovely, a piano chord, a guitar string plucked, a saxophone note ... none of these make music until there is a silence among the notes, a space that allows another sound, another note, to manifest.

And it is exactly so with the mind. Although we are likely to say that it is the thoughts that make the mind what it is, it is actually the silence among the thoughts that constructs your mind.

> "When we meditate, what we do is enter into a vacant, calm, still, silent mind. We go deep within and approach our true existence."
> **Sri Chinmoy**

Meditation is conscious intention of silence among the thoughts. The more one meditates, the more one hears the music of the mind arise among the sounds. This leads to insights, knowing, intuition, peace, happiness, and enlightenment.

Just like it is challenging to learn to play an instrument, it can be challenging to learn to still the mind, to meditate. But the more we do it, the more proficient we become, moving forward to ever more challenging and longer pieces of music, or perhaps, even, to writing one's own songs.

And, again, this is so with meditation, experiencing different forms and longer periods of meditation, and discovering one's own "music" and "muse." You will find the spaces between the sounds of the mind, and in that peaceful place, you'll discover your true self.

Today's *Way to Excellent Life* is to simply sit quietly. Any way that is comfortable is fine, but it can be helpful to connect (ground) with the earth, so sitting cross-legged on the floor may be beneficial in connecting with intention. After you have situated your body so that you are comfortable, simply sit quietly for ten minutes. Longer is fine if you're inclined. Notice the thoughts that come up and just brush them away for now, and consider the space between the notes.

> *"Meditation creates more time than it takes."*
> **Peter McWilliams**

Write in your book your experiences with meditation. You'll perhaps be surprised with the brilliance of insights that may come up to the surface of the pond of your mind, when the surface is calm even for a few moments.

Meditate every day, and before long, you will discover the music in your own mind.

> *"A calm mind is not disturbed by the waves of thoughts."*
> **Remez Sasson**

41

PEOPLE

What is the single thing you most like about people?

Explore this contemplation and write about it in your book.

42

CREATORS

We've been created to create, so do not hesitate to manifest your creations.

Honor yourself and your Heart's Desire. Reside in the Field of Dreams where you dream the dreams of your own creations, where your creations have come into being and contribute to moving forward the human quest.

Your creations may be small, they may be huge. This is not a quest of "size," it's laying claim to manifesting that which is calling to you.

Do you ever have a sense of purpose, or know that you have a calling? Don't ignore this sense, this knowing. Investigate it and allow it to blossom.

Only you have come to this three-dimensional existence with your gifts. It doesn't matter if your gifts are similar to someone else's. Your creations are unique in that it's not only what you are creating, but also the entire environment in which you create, all the components make your creation unique.

> *"Unless you try to do something beyond what you have already, mastered, you will never grow."*
> **Ralph Waldo Emerson**

What your talents, skills, insights and drive urge you to create does not occur in a vacuum. Your gifts will ignite an awareness among those who can hear you. Release the notion that someone else is already doing, or has already done, what you would do.

Simply, *DO* what you would do, for those who will hear you, see you, understand you.

> *"When we create something, we always create it first in a thought form. If we are positive in attitude, expecting and envisioning pleasure, satisfaction and happiness, we will attract and create people, situations, and events which conform to our positive expectations."*
> **Shakti Gawain**

We are each in our own unique location in time, space, consciousness, and "cosmic web" point.

Each of us has the potential to make a node of light on that web, which lights up and advances every one of us on our composite journey.

Do not judge the size or color or intensity or shape of your light. Just accept the assignment of lighting it and manifesting your creations. A song, a garden, a poem, a drawing, a city, a building, a study of dolphin language, psychic awareness, so on and so forth. Whatever your creative calling, respond!

> *"Make every thought ... that comes into your mind ... work for you. Think of things not as they are but as they might be. Don't merely dream - but create!"*
> **Robert Collier**

For today's *Way to Excellent Life* write in your book about one creative aspiration you've had that you have not begun to manifest. Write what it will look like when accomplished in a simple one or two sentence statement. Then work from that statement back toward the present moment, noting the small steps you see yourself taking, in reverse order.

The first statement is the result, what happens just before that? And then, just before that?

Now number these actions from the present moment forward. Consider the call to action expressed in number one. Affirm to yourself that you are attending to your calling, that you are going to manifest your creations, and that nothing will get in the way.

The universe is holding its breath, so to speak, to see your creations!

> *"You're in a battle between the limits of a crowd seeking the surrender of your dreams, and the power of your true vision to create and contribute. It is a fight between those who will tell you what you cannot do, and that part of you that knows, and has always known, that a dream, backed by an unrelenting will to attain it, is ... a reality with an imminent arrival."*
> **Anthony Robbins**

43

GENEROSITY

Be generous in word and deed. Give compliments with the same openness as gifts. Give gifts for no apparent reason.

> *"Happiness, freedom, peace of mind are all obtained by giving them away."*
> **Peyton Conway March**

Why not be lavish in your compliments? If you admire someone's hair or blouse, or suit or shoes or pleasant frame of mind, say so.

If a co-worker comes up with a good idea or worked hard on a project, why not tell her and let her know that you appreciate her contribution to the mutual commitment.

Is not all work of everyone ultimately contributions to our mutual, human, commitment?

Giving is the most edifying means of receiving that there is. Being generous is being open. It's impossible to hand someone something that belonged to you, and now belongs to them, without sharing a piece of yourself.

> *"You might experiment with using the cultivation of generosity as a vehicle for deep self-observation and inquiry — as well as an exercise in giving."*
> **Jon Kabat-Zin**

Your energy is attached to everything you possess, so whether openly giving something to someone, or quietly and anonymously putting a box of goodies in the Goodwill drop off, add a blessing to the box, and affirm that the items find their new owners, and that the new owners are blessed by coming in contact with your gift.

> *"Do all the good you can,
> by all the means you can,
> in all the ways you can,
> in all the places you can,
> at all the times you can,
> to all the people you can,
> as long as ever you can."*
> **John Wesley**

Experience gratitude for the generous plenty in your life that allows you the privilege to give good things to others.

Today look in your closet, or through your books, or in the kitchen drawers and find at least one attractive or interesting or useful item to give away. You may discover that a few items jump right into your hands.

> *"You make a living by what you get.*
> *You make a life by what you give away."*
> **Winston Churchill**

The number of items is not the focus, nor is the notion of the value of the items the focus—your *intention* is the focus.

The intention is to give openheartedly and openhandedly, blessing the item. Picture someone unknown to you, whom you may never meet, happily discovering this item, saying to themselves, "oh, I can really use this! What a find!"

Make in the present moment that future moment, touched with blessing and generosity.

> *"Be an opener of doors for such*
> *as come after thee."*
> **Ralph Waldo Emerson**

There is also the privilege of giving money. Giving money with an intention of generously assisting and improving the comfort, peace and joy of the human family is a most rewarding experience.

> *"Money is like manure; it's not worth a thing unless it's spread around encouraging things to grow."*
> **Thorton Wilder**

Write in your book what you see when you look about you, observing how very much you have, and how extremely blessed you are.

Write about how it feels to be so blessed and to generously give.

> *"Thousands of candles can be lit from a single candle, and the life of the candle will not be shortened. Happiness never decreases by being shared."*
> **The Buddha**

44

LOVE

All of the roads coming into and that circumference an *Excellent Life* are paved with love.

What is love?: It is care, attention, thoughtfulness, lightness in being, patience, a sensation in the body of expansion—these sensations, also known as feelings, and also emotions are but a few of love's attributes.

> "There is only a single magic,
> a single power, a single salvation
> and that is called loving."
> **Hermann Hesse**

As long as love is at the core of your actions, thoughts, motivations, intentions, drives, inspirations and creations, all of these energies will manifest, whole and life changing. Wholeness is always present when you leave all to love.

Think now of some activity or someone or some creature you love. The objective is to bring to mind a love feeling that has nothing to do with romantic emotion or sensations, but a purely unconditional love, which Buddhists call "metta." Attend to the sensations in your body when you think of this person, creature, activity, or object.

Notice that you have a pleasant sense of expansion in your chest or solar plexus which radiates into your limbs. The goal is to have that state of being at your core at all times.

> "To the extent you know love, you become love. Love is more than an emotion. It is a force of nature and therefore must contain truth. The purest love lies where it is least expected—in unattachment."
> **Depak Chopra**

Focusing on love, and becoming aware of the bodily and mind sensations and thoughts that love induces, will manifest within you this overall state of pleasant expansion habitually.

Create a habit of love!

> "Love will not be constrained by mastery; when mastery comes, the God of love at once beats his wings, and farewell, he is gone."
> **Chaucer**

Write in your book your experience of the sensation when you contemplated agape love.

Whenever you feel out of sorts, you can teach yourself to recall and induce this peaceful, energized and contented bodily sensation, which will be accompanied by the pleasant emotional state of being.

> "We have a great capacity for love, friendship, generosity, kindness, faith, hope and joy."
> **Dean Koontz**

Revisit what you wrote about how the expanded, calming and centering sensation of love felt, which will allow it to flood you again.

Contemplate the following words of the Buddha. Within the poetry is clearly expressed the power of love, and the wonderful results if one follows the simple, and lovingly given, directions:

> *Let your love flow outward through the universe,*
> *To its height, its depth, its broad extent,*
> *A limitless love, without hatred or enmity.*
>
> *Then as you stand or walk,*
> *Sit or lie down,*
> *As long as you are awake,*
> *Strive for this with a one-pointed mind;*
> *Your life will bring heaven to earth.*
> **The Buddha**

45 Ways To Excellent Life

Celebrating My Insights

45

CELEBRATE!

Now, look over your no longer blank book and find some occasions where you wrote "I don't know," or left blanks.

Write some things that you now know that you didn't know before, reference the page and subject of the previous "not knowing" and date the present entry.

Celebrate your life, full of empowerment and the ability to learn, gain insights, to be kind to yourself, acquire wisdom, have patience, imagine creatively, think deeply, and, above all, be filled with Gratitude and Unconditional Love!

Thank You ....

for reading **45 Ways to Excellent Life**. Enter the following web address if you would like a gift of several posters from my book, ***Life Flows on the River of Love***:

http://eepurl.com/cKLPxn

*May All Things Bright & Beautiful
Fill Your Days
& Dreams of Joy
Fill Your Nights!*

About the Author

It's about You—but here's a few words about me to inspire your trust in what I write ....

I know that a happy, kind, productive world evolves from happy, kind, productive, individual people.

The goal of my writing is to help clear your path to joyful productivity, in the glow of a healthy, contented, and meaningful life.

A Bit of Bio ....
I received my Doctorate from the University of California at Irvine in the School of Social Sciences, with a focus on psychology and ethnography. I've always been relentlessly curious about how people think, and how those thoughts make them feel.

After I submitted my doctoral dissertation, I moved to the Pacific Northwest, to write and to have a small private psychotherapy practice in a tiny town not much bigger than a village.

I worked with many amazing people, and witnessed astounding emotional, psychological, and spiritual, healing. It was a wonderful experience. But after twenty plus years, I realized it was time to put my focus on my writing, wherein I could potentially help greater numbers of people. Where I could meet you!

I live on ten acres of forest with a few domestic and numerous wild creatures. Along with creating an ever-growing inventory of books, my writing has appeared in hundreds of online and print publications.

Your support of my writing helps support ten acres of natural forest, and all its resident fauna. All the creatures and I thank you!

Questions, comments, observations, reviews? I'd love to hear from you!:
Blythe@BlytheAyne.com

www.BlytheAyne.com

www.ingramcontent.com/pod-product-compliance
Lightning Source LLC
Chambersburg PA
CBHW021441080526
44588CB00009B/633